NATO Partnerships and the Arab Spring: Achievements and Perspectives for the 2012 Chicago Summit

NATO Partnerships and the Arab Spring: Achievements and Perspectives for the 2012 Chicago Summit

By Isabelle François

Center for Transatlantic Security Studies
Institute for National Strategic Studies
Transatlantic Perspectives, No. 1

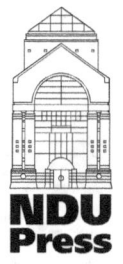

National Defense University Press
Washington, D.C.
December 2011

First printing, December 2011

For current publications of the Institute for National Strategic Studies, please go to the National Defense University Web site at: www.ndu.edu/inss.

Contents

Executive Summary

In November 2010, heads of state and government at the Lisbon Summit called for a "streamlining" of North Atlantic Treaty Organization (NATO) partnerships. In early 2011, the Alliance developed a more flexible and efficient partnership policy. It did so in accordance with the Lisbon tasking, and prepared simultaneously for a new mission, with contributions from several partner countries, as events unfolded in Libya. These developments involved significant NATO consultation with partner countries.

This July 2011 paper highlights the synergy between the new policy and NATO's response to the Libyan crisis. It points to some of the challenges facing the Alliance in the context of Operation *Unified Protector*, and in further developing NATO partnerships with countries south of the Mediterranean. The paper, written well before fast-moving political and military events significantly altered the situation in Libya, offers recommendations in preparation for the next NATO summit so as to make best use of Alliance partnerships if the Allies decide to build on the Libyan operation and develop a new strategic direction in the face of the tumultuous political transition in the Arab world south of the Mediterranean.

Building on the Achievements of the Lisbon Summit

Six months prior to the November 2010 Lisbon Summit, a group of experts chaired by Madeleine Albright provided an independent report entitled *NATO 2020: Assured Security; Dynamic Engagement* to the NATO Secretary-General.[1] This report was developed in response to the Secretary-General's expressed desire to consult prior to launching the internal drafting process of the 2010 Strategic Concept within NATO. The Alliance was struck by the importance devoted to NATO partnerships in the report. In turn, the Strategic Concept raised the profile of partnerships by elevating cooperative security to the level of "essential core tasks" for the Alliance—one of the three tasks alongside collective security and crisis management.[2] NATO heads of state and government at the Lisbon Summit, while adopting the Strategic Concept, also devoted particular attention to partnerships in their own Summit Declaration.[3] They reiterated the commitment to developing political dialogue and practical cooperation with NATO partners, and directed the North Atlantic Council to develop "a more efficient and flexible partnership policy" in time for the April 2011 Foreign Ministers' meeting in Berlin.[4]

On April 15, 2011, in Berlin, NATO Foreign Ministers endorsed the new partnership policy developed and agreed with partners.[5] In essence, this policy document provided for increased flexibility in using NATO partnership tools and mechanisms now at the disposal of all partners beyond those of Partnership for Peace.[6] It also allowed for increased consultation in flexible formats potentially available to all NATO partners, and possibly other significant interlocutors on issues of common concerns. Finally, it provided for a more structured role for partner countries contributing to NATO-led operations. This came at a time when partners from the south were closely consulted in the context of Operation *Unified Protector*.

In developing the Lisbon agenda, Allies had not anticipated the dramatic events that were to unfold in the southern rim of the Mediterranean, sweeping countries from Egypt to Libya in the spring of 2011. A wind of political change led to regional upheaval and ultimately to armed conflict, resulting in a new NATO-led operation in the particular case of Libya. In responding to the Libyan crisis, NATO, following its March 27 decision,[7] immediately reached out to all of its partners formally in an extended format beyond the Euro-Atlantic Partnership Council and, informally, through quiet diplomacy between the leadership of NATO and partner representatives. NATO was particularly interested in the contribution and support from its Arab partners.[8] In this context, the Alliance relied on its existing partnership frameworks with countries of the Mediterranean Dialogue (MD)[9] and those of the Istanbul Cooperation Initiative (ICI)[10] for the Persian Gulf region, which had often been criticized in the past for a lack of vision and limited

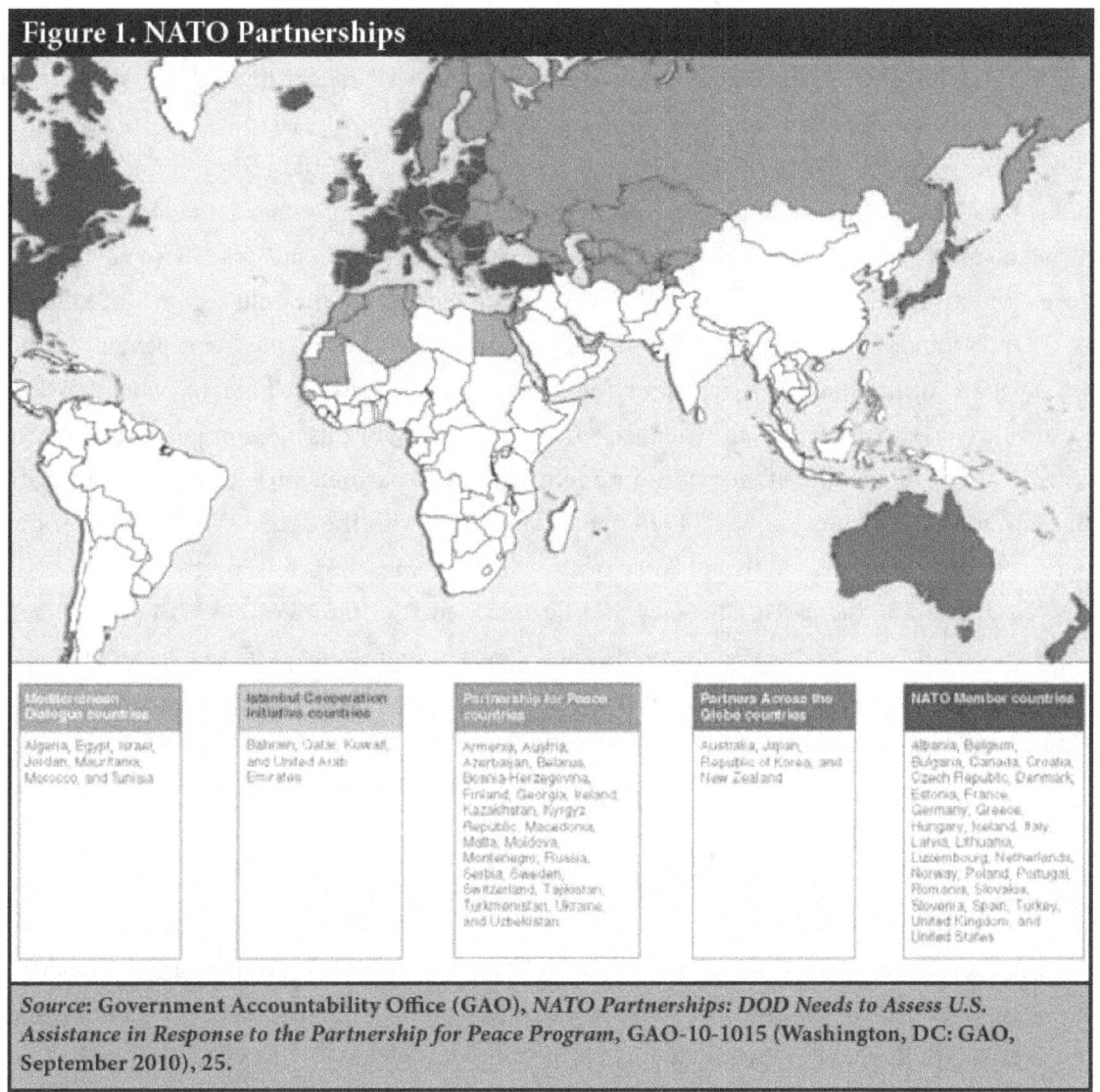

Figure 1. NATO Partnerships

Mediterranean Dialogue countries	Istanbul Cooperation Initiative countries	Partnership for Peace countries	Partners Across the Globe countries	NATO Member countries
Algeria, Egypt, Israel, Jordan, Mauritania, Morocco, and Tunisia	Bahrain, Qatar, Kuwait, and United Arab Emirates	Armenia, Austria, Azerbaijan, Belarus, Bosnia-Herzegovina, Finland, Georgia, Ireland, Kazakhstan, Kyrgyz Republic, Macedonia, Malta, Moldova, Montenegro, Russia, Serbia, Sweden, Switzerland, Tajikistan, Turkmenistan, Ukraine, and Uzbekistan	Australia, Japan, Republic of Korea, and New Zealand	Albania, Belgium, Bulgaria, Canada, Croatia, Czech Republic, Denmark, Estonia, France, Germany, Greece, Hungary, Iceland, Italy, Latvia, Lithuania, Luxembourg, Netherlands, Norway, Poland, Portugal, Romania, Slovakia, Slovenia, Spain, Turkey, United Kingdom, and United States

Source: Government Accountability Office (GAO), *NATO Partnerships: DOD Needs to Assess U.S. Assistance in Response to the Partnership for Peace Program*, GAO-10-1015 (Washington, DC: GAO, September 2010), 25.

concrete results in the area of defense cooperation failing to bind these partners to the Alliance.[11] And yet these partnerships proved most useful as Allies needed to consult quickly and decisively to gain the necessary political and military support to engage effectively in the region as it deployed Operation *Unified Protector*.[12] The Alliance thus reaffirmed the importance of its partnerships in practice, as it was finalizing its new partnership policy.

In the light of events and the so-called Arab Spring, some already argue that there may be scope for increased NATO interest in the south, and possible new demands in the near future from its southern partners.[13] NATO's new engagement in the south was certainly not a political design from the Lisbon Summit; it was the result of unforeseen circumstances, quickly met by

NATO's ability to respond to new political-military requirements in the face of events unfolding in a region where the Alliance counted a number of well-established relations. Interestingly enough, developments on the ground and NATO's ability to reach out to partners in the context of Operation *Unified Protector* reinforced the objective of the Lisbon Summit, which called for a "more efficient and flexible partnership policy," streamlining partnership tools and mechanisms, opening them to all, and enhancing consultation mechanisms. These new policy developments might become of particular relevance to partners of the Gulf region and MD.

One should, however, resist the temptation to interpret recent Allies' engagement in the region as the prime result of a new direction in NATO's partnerships. In fact, such a decision would likely be divisive within the Alliance.[14] If anything, these events have provided the context for reinforcing the validity of a longstanding commitment to partnership within the Alliance, its significance in the context of NATO-led operations, along with the necessity to preserve some of its core principles, such as that of "specificity" when it comes to various partnerships.

In developing increased efficiency and flexibility for the future of NATO partnerships, while consulting with partners on their roles and contributions in the particular case of Operation *Unified Protector*, Allies were reminded of two longstanding premises of partnership: first, NATO operations cannot be conceived without the contributions of partners; and, second, each region and partnership has its own dynamic and requires a tailored approach.

Preparing for the 2012 Chicago Summit

While some partners will be invited to join the International Security Assistance Force meeting as troop-contributing nations to the NATO-led operation in Afghanistan, others will be in attendance for specific meetings that may also take place in the context of this summit—be it a meeting of the NATO-Russia Council, a meeting of the NATO-Ukraine Commission, or a meeting of the NATO-Georgia Council. All partner heads of state and government may be gathered in a meeting of the Euro-Atlantic Partnership Council with their allied counterparts. Alternatively—or perhaps in addition—as foreseen in Lisbon, and in accordance with the Lisbon Declaration,[15] a larger number of heads of state and government, possibly from BRICS (Brazil, Russia, India, China, South Africa) countries could conceivably join the summit as significant interlocutors in today's security environment.

It is too early to tell who will be invited to the NATO Summit and what will be on the agenda of the various meetings. Nonetheless, it is safe to assume that the NATO-led operation in Libya and its consequences on NATO partnerships could generate widespread interest and loom large in the summit preparations. Moreover, the Chicago Summit will take place back-to-back with the Group of Eight (G8) Summit. In the context of the G8 event, there may be a meeting of the G8 + 5, which would bring Brazil, China, India, Mexico, and South Africa around the G8 table. BRICS representatives, therefore, could be present in the United States at the time of the NATO Summit and could conceivably be invited to join a "big tent event" to discuss the lessons learned from the Libyan crisis and exchange views with Allies on potential common security challenges emanating from the southern shore of the Mediterranean.

This paper presents the case for hosting a "big tent meeting" in Chicago, bringing NATO partners along with new interlocutors from countries to organizations, which may have an interest in discussing with NATO its current commitment to Libya and exchange views on peace and stability in North Africa and the Gulf region in the wake of the Arab Spring. At the same time, the paper points to some serious challenges facing both the Alliance internally, as well as NATO partnerships, in developing such an agenda based on Operation *Unified Protector* and NATO's potential role beyond the Libyan crisis. While the paper recognizes the benefit of a "more efficient and flexible partnership policy" developed in the wake of the Lisbon Summit, and the possibility to build on these achievements to enhance relations with countries from the MD and the ICI, it cautions against the pitfalls of a new strategic direction which would take NATO farther south,[16] and stresses the need to reach out to other significant security interlocutors, if it is to develop a balanced role south of the Mediterranean.

NATO Looking South?

The Challenge of Maintaining Consensus

NATO's engagement in Libya, despite its sound legal and political basis, has faced significant challenges in terms of internal cohesion and external pressure on the Alliance. While the current mandate for the NATO-led operation in Libya has been renewed until the end of September 2011,[17] different political interests within the Alliance in the face of the Libyan conflict have proven particularly challenging. From the early days of consultations within NATO, prior to the March 27 decision to launch Operation *Unified Protector*, differences of approach and diverging political interests on the part of various Allies, notably France, Germany, and Turkey, did not escape the media.[18] Again in June, consensus was challenged immediately following the meeting of NATO Defense Ministers, which reiterated the Alliance's agreement to stay the course and keep up the pressure until NATO goals were achieved.[19] Days after the NATO meeting on June 22, Italian Foreign Minister Franco Frattini called for an immediate suspension of the campaign in the face of civilian casualties in the wake of NATO airstrikes to allow for humanitarian aid to reach people in need.[20] This reversal of position was confirmed 2 days later by Prime Minister Silvio Berlusconi, who pushed toward political mediation at a European Union (EU) Summit on June 24 to deliver a final solution to the Libyan crisis. Some may argue that this has more to do with internal Italian politics than civilian casualties, but the point is that consensus around the NATO-led operation cannot be taken for granted.

For as long as public opinion has supported allied military engagement against the forces of Muammar Qadhafi, consensus within NATO was likely to be maintained.[21] It is worth noting that Italy has been the country whose public was most opposed to the hostilities in Libya, hence the Italian government's show of impatience. Since France seemed the least challenged by its own public opinion and domestic opposition, it has been able to shoulder a leading role in the air campaign, which suited well President Nicolas Sarkozy and his political ambitions, giving him an opportunity to appear as a strong leader in the run up to the 2012 presidential election. In any event, time is not on NATO's side, and the longer Libyan internal hostilities persist in the absence of final political settlement and a stabilization process, the more challenging it is for the Alliance to maintain consensus and ultimately to preserve support and credibility in the region for long-term partnership activities.

Various governments engaged in diplomatic talks in search of a political solution to the Libyan crisis—from France, United Kingdom, the United States, Italy, Turkey, and others within the Alliance, to the Russian Federation and others outside the Alliance. The lack of a unified diplomatic approach, despite the existence of the Libya Contact Group,[22] generated some confusion in the face of numerous initiatives often competing with one another. While there was consensus on the need for an immediate ceasefire, initiatives varied in terms of which Libyan parties to involve in the process of reaching a political settlement.[23] The Transitional National Council (TNC) opposing Qadhafi forces was inimical to any negotiated settlement—which would have allowed Qadhafi to stay in Libya—and looked for nothing short of expelling him and his close entourage.[24]

Final settlement in Libya months into the NATO-led operation is still pending. In spite of international attempts at a negotiated settlement between Qadhafi forces and the so-called TNC rebels, this proved impossible. The TNC takeover of Tripoli in mid-August put an end to this option. The rebels will now have to prepare for transition in Libya ensuring inclusive political representation in future government institutions and the electoral process, while guaranteeing territorial integrity. This will likely take months, and NATO will remain engaged abiding by its commitments until the TNC decides with the international community on the requirements after Operation *Unified Protector*.

In this volatile environment, NATO has maneuvered in a precarious situation. It has had to carry forward an operation in the face of a fragile consensus, but without direct leverage in the diplomatic search for a political settlement. Moreover, it has had to rely on bilateral efforts from some of its member states and on broader efforts from the international community. A postconflict settlement among various Libyan entities may be reached prior to the Chicago Summit. However, its sustainability and the follow-on reconstruction in Libya will most likely remain on the agenda of the international community, with a likely yet undefined supporting role for NATO in this transition process well beyond the summit. In this context, a "big tent meeting" in Chicago would provide Allies with an opportunity to review NATO's role and strategy in Libya and offer a broader forum to exchange views on lessons learned from Operation *Unified Protector* involving key interlocutors in the field of security who voted in support of the United Nations Security Council Resolution (UNSCR) 1973, yet not necessarily in support of the NATO-led operation as it unfolded. Reaching out to these countries will also provide an opportunity to look beyond the NATO-led operation into future support to the broader effort of the international community, as it may be called upon to support the TNC in its transition efforts toward reconstruction in this war-torn society.

Working Toward a Comprehensive Approach

Transition to a successful political settlement has always been a thorny issue in crisis management. NATO has often argued in the context of its operations that a military solution alone does not suffice to manage today's complex crises and operations, and has urged the international community to work together toward a "comprehensive approach" to addressing current operations and reconstructions efforts.[25] The NATO-led Operation *Unified Protector* showed progress in terms of NATO's partnership with other international and regional organizations. Recent institutional gains in developing the political will and working out mechanisms for consultation between organizations proved most useful. While it was still fresh and habits of consultation had not yet set in, the NATO Secretary-General was able to quickly establish contacts with his counterparts and engage in high diplomacy in the context of the NATO March 27 decision to take on the whole military operation in Libya in implementation of UNSCR 1973. Within hours and over the first few days, contacts were established with the UN, EU, Arab League, African Union, Gulf Cooperation Council, and others such as the Office for the Coordination of Humanitarian Affairs at the highest level. This was handled in the spirit of a comprehensive approach requiring "all actors to contribute in a concerted effort, based on a shared sense of responsibility, openness and determination and taking into account their respective strengths, mandate and roles, as well as their decision-making autonomy."[26]

In terms of NATO's comprehensive approach, much progress has been achieved at the leadership level. In the context of the Libyan crisis, heads of international organizations quickly shared information and reached out to each other in times of emergency, bringing the value-added of each organization to bear in search of a political settlement. That said, as the Libyan case will likely show, the shift from a military operation to political settlement as well as reconstruction efforts remains a challenge, and will require constant and thorough efforts to integrate the necessary action, coordination, and transition from military to civilian efforts.

The Libyan case has already demonstrated the challenge in mobilizing and preparing for postconflict leadership beyond the NATO-led operation. The NATO Secretary-General at the June NATO meeting of Defense Ministers called on the international community, the Libyan contact group, and other civilian organizations to start investing in this transition.[27] The ultimate challenge that Operation *Unified Protector* will likely show in the months to come will lie in the transition from an operational environment to that of a reconstruction phase. To that end, it will continue to be important for NATO to develop new capabilities and mechanisms to reach out to civilians and the private sector.

Peacetime efforts on the part of NATO strategic commanders (Supreme Allied Commander Europe and Supreme Allied Commander Transformation) should be pursued, thereby enhancing allied capabilities to respond to crises and further operationalize the concept of a comprehensive approach. These efforts include integrating training and education and developing the necessary modules/packages to deploy military forces, humanitarian relief assistance, and other civilian contributions, including capabilities from the private sector to ensure smoother transition to postconflict efforts.

Different political interests from one international organization to another will remain and continue to create challenges in terms of partnership between organizations. At the same time, these diverging interests may enrich the international community by providing additional options in developing a necessary political settlement to a particular crisis. While diversity is challenging when building consensus, it may prove to be an asset in terms of political settlement. The Libyan crisis may benefit, for instance, from the differences of approach in the African Union and Gulf Cooperation Council. The former was originally amenable to finding a political settlement, which included Qadhafi, while the latter was more inclined to search for a solution that excluded the challenged leader and his entourage. The Libyan crisis and its outcome will ultimately have an impact for both Arabs and Africans alike. Africa has traditionally been a place for long debates in search of consensus, where everyone has a voice and has to be heard. One can build on this tradition.

In that context, a big tent event in Chicago that brings the relevant organizations and interested parties (beyond well-established partners and troop contributors) would offer a useful forum to enhance dialogue toward sustaining a much needed political settlement on the ground in Libya. Moreover, it would position NATO as an important player among many, and put in context the Alliance's decision to intervene militarily in Libya on March 27, addressing the concerns of those who see in NATO's decision a desire to "expand south."

NATO Partnerships and the South

Reaching Beyond Existing Membership Within Partnership Frameworks

The political and military support of Arab and African countries beyond the partnership relations that bind NATO to its MD and ICI partners will be crucial. There is currently a clear divide between the 11 countries in North Africa and the Gulf region that have established relations with NATO and those who did not join these frameworks. Opposition to NATO-led operation in the region from countries outside of the NATO partnership frameworks, such as Oman, will need to be taken into consideration in order to develop a balanced approach to the NATO-led operation in Libya. It is worth noting that Libya itself was not among NATO's 11 partners south of the Mediterranean. As in the case of Iraq and Afghanistan, it is likely that NATO will eventually look to develop a long-term partnership with Libya beyond Operation *Unified Protector*. There may be scope for engaging in a dialogue with countries that may have refrained from or opposed partnership with the Alliance until now, but that cannot be excluded from NATO's involvement in the region if the Alliance has to develop a balanced approach to developments in North Africa and the Gulf region.

There is also a clear divide among the 11 NATO partners from the south, which has proved challenging at times—notwithstanding the fact that existing frameworks were most useful in the early days of the crisis as NATO decided to deploy Operation *Unified Protector*. Indeed, differences of opinion were quickly apparent among African and Arab partners with countries of the Gulf considering the Libyan crisis an "Arab" issue rather than an African one. These differences were mirrored in the approach of the African Union to the Libyan crisis compared to that of the Gulf Cooperation Council. The region south of the Mediterranean is far from homogeneous. In fact, the MD and ICI have not resulted in vibrant cooperative frameworks in the past, in part due to their lack of common purpose and common approach to security challenges. Internal divisions within these groups of countries and between NATO partners and neighboring countries harboring misgivings vis-à-vis NATO recall the limits of these partnerships.[28] That said, some representatives from the Gulf region

(ICI partners) during consultations with NATO in the early days of Operation *Unified Protector* were quick to point out the need to gain African support. Thus, enhanced and inclusive political dialogue may have to be further developed as the Alliance considers a broader cooperative role in the region.

While there may be scope for enhancing political dialogue and reaching out beyond the membership of MD and ICI in search for broader common understandings between NATO and partners south of the Mediterranean, practical cooperation with these countries may still be challenging in the near term. First, as already mentioned, the MD and ICI have yielded limited results in terms of practical cooperation. The Arab Spring may have changed the political reality for a number of NATO partners in the region and may ultimately affect partners' interest in what NATO has to offer to assist them in the face of political changes in their societies, but they are not yet "*demandeurs*." Second, practical cooperation may not be as important as political dialogue in the immediate aftermath of Operation *Unified Protector*. A broader exchange of views in search of common understandings may become more relevant, as exchanging information, building trust, and assessing risks and threats as perceived by different parties will be required to assist countries in defining how to best address the Arab Spring and search for common responses to common challenges.

Challenges and Opportunities of "Specific" Partnerships in Addressing Political Transition in Countries South of the Mediterranean

Beyond political dialogue, practical cooperation will always be an option if required. Over the past 15 years, NATO has accumulated considerable experience in assisting partners of Central and Eastern Europe in their defense-related transformation agendas. The Alliance could easily draw on its tools and mechanisms. It could draw, for instance, from its Individual Partnership Action Plan to assist a partner interested in creating its own defense within a democratic system of checks and balances that has a modern administration and accountable planning, budgeting, and resources management. NATO could also draw from its Planning and Review Process to assist a partner in modernizing its armed forces, building the necessary capabilities for defense transformation, allowing for a transfer of best practices in the area of defense planning and budgeting, possibly assisting also in the "demilitarization" of some of the security sector administrations, and developing modern personnel management systems.

Through partnership, NATO has developed expertise over the years, promoted good practices in civilian control and oversight of the military, and addressed issues of corruption in the security sector, notably through its Building Integrity Initiative. Partnering with nongovernmental organizations, such as Transparency International, NATO experts are able to provide assistance in developing transparency, accountability, and integrity in the security sector, thereby assisting in the development of good governance. It should be noted that this type of assistance—based on a shared interest in "good governance" rather than on "democratic values" that originally bound Allies to their partners of Central and Eastern Europe—might be a more appropriate base for future cooperative projects with partners south of the Mediterranean.

Perhaps even more relevant for NATO's southern partners in the long term, the Alliance has devoted significant efforts to training and education programs. These programs provide partners with required assistance from professional educators to develop their cadres in the armed forces, thereby assisting in the design of their own curriculum to teach their military and security forces. At times, NATO also provided simple expertise to a particular group of countries, such as the South East Europe Security Cooperation Steering Group (SEEGROUP), favoring a process owned and directed by a group of countries rather than negotiated with individual partners.

Countries of North Africa and the Gulf region, however, are not Central and Eastern Europe. They are not bound by a common objective to join the Alliance. There is no need for NATO to assist North African or Gulf countries in preparing for membership. There is not even the indirect incentive of EU membership toward which NATO could contribute. But there is potentially a useful contribution that NATO could make to African and Arab partner countries: helping them build their own capacities. A specific demand from a partner country or regional organization would have to be forthcoming. It should not be excluded that countries in North Africa and the Gulf region decide to focus in the future on their own regional means and ability to deal with a particular crisis.[29]

In the short term, Arab countries facing political transition from North Africa to the Gulf region are unlikely to be rushing to NATO for a miraculous transition package. Governments facing uprisings and challenges to their authority will be confronted first and foremost by socioeconomic realities. Neighboring countries will be affected by migration flux and potential refugee crises as uprisings persist. Calls on the international community for assistance to transition governments would likely be in the socioeconomic sphere, addressing organizations such as the International Monetary Fund and World Bank, UN agencies, African Development Bank, or European Union. Assistance in civilian institution-building to face elections, the independence of the judiciary and legislatures, along with calls to ensure border security, will likely be given priority over defense and security reform.

NATO may still have a particular role to play beyond the NATO-led operation in the near term as it prepares for the Chicago Summit. It could enhance political dialogue by reaching out broadly to pave the way for possible practical cooperation in the long run, assuming there is an interest south of the Mediterranean to partner with NATO beyond Operation *Unified Protector*. The operation in Libya will likely have far-reaching consequences on the Alliance's ability to develop a genuine partnership with countries of North Africa and the Gulf region. While it is too early to draw conclusions on the consequences of the operation, one can safely assume that an inclusive dialogue will be necessary to explain NATO to North Africans and to populations in the Gulf region in order to nurture political contacts at the highest levels. In the wake of Operation *Unified Protector*, NATO will have to reach out more broadly to countries in the region beyond its MD and ICI partners, as one does not win many hearts through air strikes even in the case of a successful outcome.

Despite 15 to 20 years of NATO partnerships in various regions—in North Africa, the Gulf region, Central and Eastern Europe, Central Asia, even reaching beyond to "partners around the globe"—the Alliance has not dispelled longstanding misperceptions about its roles and policies in today's security environment, at times even prompting questions about its raison d'être 20 years after the end of the Cold War. In many ways, NATO's image south of the Mediterranean is close to the perception prevailing in Russia and essentially plagued by a fundamental lack of trust.

Practical cooperation with skeptical partners has not yielded mutual understanding. Despite concrete programs of courses, training, exercises, and visits over the years aimed at military-to-military cooperation, political dialogue has lagged behind with these partners falling short of developing common views and addressing differences of threat perceptions. Skepticism has hampered some partners in developing the necessary trust for cooperation to take root. As NATO prepares for the Chicago Summit and looks beyond the 2012 horizon, the task in partnership will be to seek and develop relations with countries that may not want to embrace NATO yet, but who still recognize that the Alliance is a key player in today's security environment. These countries may be prepared to develop a partnership with NATO in search of common approaches to common challenges despite major differences on fundamental issues, basically "agreeing to disagree" on some issues while cooperating on others. The NATO-Russia partnership may offer some insights into this type of partnership.

In the context of the Libyan crisis, and irrespective of the NATO-Russia so-called strategic partnership, the Russian position has been critical of allied efforts in Operation *Unified Protector*, with Prime Minister Vladimir Putin comparing the operation to "medieval crusades."[30] The Russian president, for his part, showed some moderation in his comments recalling publicly that the military operation was sanctioned by the international community and aimed at protecting civilians from Qadhafi-led forces.[31] However, as time went by and casualties started to make the headlines, Russia stressed the importance of an immediate ceasefire and engaged in mediation in search of national reconciliation in Libya, nominating its own special envoy of the Russian president for the region, Mikhail Margelov. Recognizing the legitimacy of UNSCR 1973 and the political and operational support of a number of countries in North Africa and the Gulf region, Russian leadership was hard pressed to forcefully criticize NATO. Nonetheless, Foreign Minister Sergey Lavrov gave an interview to Bloomberg June 1 in which he did not shy away from accusing Western powers of misusing "all necessary means" in the context of UNSCR 1973, stating that they were "going far beyond the declared goal and the purposes of the resolution, and beyond the original request of the Arab League."[32]

One could have argued, however, that as the international community was looking for a negotiated settlement, the Russian government was well positioned to contribute to these efforts,[33] with an approach similar to the African Union aimed at mediating between rebel forces and the Qadhafi regime, balancing between Tripoli and Benghazi to ensure territorial integrity and a national solution. According to Minister Lavrov, Russian mediation was in fact mandated or at least sanctioned by the G8 Summit in France at the end of May 2011, responding to an appeal from President Nicolas Sarkozy, President Barack Obama, and other summit participants.[34] Moreover, despite differences in views, the NATO-Russia Council has discussed the Libyan crisis, and during the recent NATO Secretary-General visit to Russia on July 4, 2011, President Dmitry Medvedev hosted a meeting between the Secretary-General and President Jacob Zuma of South Africa to discuss the Libyan crisis.[35] More recently, during his visit to Washington in July 2011, Minister Lavrov suggested to his American host to seek and include Chinese views on the Libyan crisis.

While the idea of a negotiated settlement in Libya failed, there is still a broad international interest in a sustainable final settlement to the Libyan crisis, which paves the way to a secure and stable Libya. After a settlement, Libya can resume its oil production and engage in reconstruction. The Chicago Summit offers an occasion to reach out to countries that may not have been invited to NATO summits before, but that may share with the Alliance a common interest today in stability and security south of the Mediterranean. Based on this common interest, NATO would effectively be reaching out to countries that may not share allied values but whose different perspectives around the summit table might help the Alliance to contribute effectively to enhanced security and stability. As Allies prepare to draw lessons from Operation *Unified Protector* and exchange views with their partners, reaching out to significant interlocutors in the security field and broadening political dialogue may be in the interest of Allies and partners alike.

Chicago 2012: Libya and the Summit Agenda

At the upcoming NATO Summit, the agenda will be dominated by the concern over allied resources at a time of defense spending cuts and the need to protect core Alliance capabilities in the face of budgetary constraints. Given the preoccupations of the host country in an election year, the overall theme of the NATO Summit will likely go more in the direction of "protecting" rather than "expanding." The summit does not have to be an inward looking event, however, mainly focused on NATO internal business. NATO-led operations will figure prominently on the agenda, and a large number of partners and other significant interlocutors in today's security environment may join Allies in Chicago.

"Smart Defense"

It is expected that one of the key themes will be "smart defense,"[36] a concept coined by the NATO Secretary-General in an attempt to identify capability areas where NATO Allies needed to keep investing and work multinationally to mitigate the decline in defense spending, and thus address some of the concerns raised last June by the outgoing U.S. Secretary of Defense Robert Gates.[37] NATO-led operations, and Operation *Unified Protector* in particular, are not irrelevant to the current NATO capability debate. First, as outlined by the Secretary-General, the NATO-led operation in Libya has shown that "in addition to frontline capabilities, such as fighter-bombers and warships, so-called enablers, such as surveillance and refueling aircraft, as well as drones, are critical parts of any modern operation."[38] As the price of military equipment rises and defense budgets decline, the Allies will have to identify what they can do jointly at a lower cost and more efficiently.

Second, Operation *Unified Protector* has woken up the Alliance to the fact that the United States may not always take the lead in future NATO-led operations. Washington is facing its own budgetary challenges, and burden-sharing within the Alliance seems more relevant than ever. This will likely push the debate on European contributions to security to the fore and into the public domain. The issue could trigger a divisive debate, insofar as European defense spending cuts may affect Europe's ability to take care of crises even at its periphery, and turn the United States slowly but surely away from the original transatlantic bargain at the heart of NATO, given American taxpayers' unlikely support for what might be perceived as unequal burden-sharing in Euro-Atlantic security.

That said, Operation *Unified Protector* has pointed to an alternative to this gloomy scenario. It may come to symbolize American success in convincing its Allies that Europeans had to take a greater share of the burden and assume greater responsibility for security in Europe's periphery. Operation *Unified Protector* has also served as a reminder that NATO is the only organization with the command and control ability to take over such a complex operation, even allowing the United States to play a pivotal but supporting role. Despite regular press reports on the lack of sufficient strike capabilities, the Alliance was still the only organization willing and able to respond swiftly to the military requirements in Libya and sustain the operation to date. It has been argued that the operation was sustained by only a small number of Allies (eight) with a few partners. However, American assets and capabilities made available to European Allies were critical. One might argue that rather than a shortage of capabilities, Allies might suffer more from political rather than military constraints. Ensuring the necessary political will from capitals to support NATO-led operations and to create consensus may be as challenging in the future as maintaining military capabilities, especially at a time of budget cuts.

In light of these considerations at the heart of NATO's decisionmaking and ability to act militarily, one might wonder whether the NATO-led operation in Libya could seriously lead to similar missions in the near future. First, the Arab Spring seems to point to more unrest looming from Arab countries in transition from Egypt to Yemen and Syria to name but a few. Social media are replete with exchanges on this issue. It also testifies to considerable uneasiness on the part of the populations with the ongoing transition process in their countries, often pointing to fear of violence as a more likely outcome than peaceful transition. Would NATO be prepared to intervene militarily elsewhere in the region based on what has so far been perceived as a NATO success in Libya? For those who thought once again that NATO intervention in Libya would be limited and quick, lessons from the past 10 to 15 years have not registered. The difficulties encountered in search of a political settlement in Libya point to the challenge facing any future military intervention in countries in the midst of political transition: it is easier to get in than to get out. The one constant in contemporary complex operations lies in their unpredictability and the need for maximum flexibility in terms of international response.

Some analysts have argued logically that the European Union should prepare to lead peacekeeping efforts in a post-Qadhafi Libya and take an operational role in its periphery in support of its Common Security and Defense Policy ambitions.[39] A UN-authorized "EU force" to be deployed for 4 to 6 months would be an option according to these analysts and would give the UN time to set up its own force. However, no one seems to volunteer on the part of the EU, and it may well be that the next crisis lands on NATO's desk in the absence of alternatives despite clear statements from Allies that there is no intention and no plan for deploying ground troops to Libya. That said, many had predicted that Afghanistan was likely to be the last NATO out of area mission, but Libya proved them wrong. Similarly, it may be too soon to conclude that there will be no other NATO-led mission in the region. In today's financial environment, the debate might point toward NATO focusing on short-term UN-mandated "bridging missions" from an open crisis to a political settlement. The outcome of Operation *Unified Protector* and the transition to reconstruction in Libya will be significant in this debate.

The transatlantic partnership embodied in NATO continues to be the main driving force in global security as the international community has witnessed in the context of the Libyan crisis. But "For how long?" asked the NATO Secretary-General in a recent article,[40] pointing to the spending gap and "relative decline of European defense spending compared to that of emerging powers and to the United States." Besides the defense spending argument, which points to China having tripled its defense spending in the last 10 years, while India increased its own by nearly 60 percent, the political argument needs to be made in support of an inclusive political dialogue involving countries such as China, India, Russia, and other emerging powers in search of political solutions to crises such as Libya. Their interest in security and stability south of the Mediterranean was clear when they allowed the United Nations Security Council to act through UNSCR 1973. Their approach and national interests may differ from that of the Euro-Atlantic community, as Russian criticisms levelled against the NATO-led operation reminded the international community. Nonetheless, the political support of emerging powers will remain essential for the Alliance, not only in the context of future UNSCRs but also in its efforts to reach sustainable political settlements in conflicts, such as the one plaguing Libya. Even though BRICS countries did not volunteer to contribute militarily and put their military might at the disposal of the coalition,[41] which intervened in Libya in March 2011, they remain potential contributors to a broader political dialogue.

"Smart Partnerships"

As NATO prepares for its next summit, Operation *Unified Protector* has already pointed to a few lessons learned. First, the operation has reminded the Alliance that consensus in the face of complex operations cannot be taken for granted, and that a NATO-led operation south of the Mediterranean, while closer to Europe than Afghanistan, will not escape the difficulty of maintaining consensus over time. Any interest within the Alliance for a new strategic direction for missions south of the Mediterranean would have to contend with the challenges of internal cohesion and consensus-building—in particular at a time of budgetary constraints. Second, security challenges emanating from the south would require a broader political dialogue reaching out beyond the membership of existing NATO partnership frameworks. The 2012 Chicago Summit may be an opportunity to engage in "smart partnerships": essentially reaching out to countries that may not share the same democratic values as the Allies or use the same approach in addressing international security challenges, but who represent interests from the broader international community and, as such, may contribute significantly to security challenges coming from North Africa and the Gulf region.

In the context of the Arab Spring, smart partnerships would argue for reaching out first to countries in North Africa and the Gulf region that have not yet shown any interest in joining the MD or ICI but that may find an interest in joining a broader dialogue in support of Arab countries facing political transition in an effort to avert military intervention.[42] Second, smart partnerships would pursue new cooperative avenues in bringing NATO and the EU closer together in an effort to help Arab countries transitioning toward new political systems and reform their security sectors, should there be an interest on the part of these challenged governments to reach out to Western institutions to assist in their reform process.[43] Third, smart partnerships in the wake of the Libyan crisis could open the way to a broader political dialogue with emerging powers, which might share an interest in a peaceful settlement of the Libyan crisis, and would welcome an opportunity to contribute to a broader security dialogue on security and stability talks in the region.

Finally, as NATO considers its strategic interests south of the Mediterranean and how to make best use of existing partnerships in support of allied contributions to peace and stability in North Africa and the Gulf region, a broad dialogue with emerging powers would be essential to inform the Alliance on broader issues of significance when dealing with the region. NATO would have to tread carefully in light of significant shifts and new power games at play in the Gulf, which will only increase in the wake of American withdrawal from Iraq. Power games between Arabs and Persians in the region, with Iran's potential influence on Shiite uprisings (as was the case in Bahrain recently), give a whole new dimension to explosive situations in various countries from Yemen to Syria, not to forget continued unrest in countries such as Egypt and others in North Africa. As NATO establishes new relationships in the southern rim of the Mediterranean, Iran's regional role and influence cannot be ignored and will call on the Alliance to be open to transparent consultations with its partners in the region and to dialogue on proliferation and missile defense as potential areas of common interest.

Moreover, the potential role of Turkey as it asserts itself as a regional power will influence NATO policy and direction with regard to the southern rim of the Mediterranean, especially in the light of American withdrawal from Iraq and limited, albeit pivotal American engagement in Libya. That said, southern Allies may have an interest in being proactive in the face of destabilizing political transition in Arab countries, but may prefer to address this challenge through bilateral relations or possibly through the European Union, as was the case in the recent past. Addressing security issues emanating from the southern rim of the Mediterranean bilaterally might help avoid any divisive debate within the Alliance between northern and southern Allies given the likely diverging interests and threat perceptions between them. Moreover, Allies would thus avoid a difficult debate on "prioritization" within partnerships as additional funding would be required to further develop southern partnerships, possibly at the expense of eastern and other partnerships. However, bilateral relations may not be the most efficient way to assist political transition in Arab countries. Moreover, what would that say about NATO's ability to respond to current threats and challenges? What would it say about the relevance of multilateralism to address today's most pressing security challenges?

To recall the words of the group of experts in their report *NATO 2020* issued a year ago, NATO is facing "a New Era of Partnerships."[44] To stay relevant in today's security environment, the Alliance has to engage with potential new partners and with emerging powers associating them to a broad dialogue in search for political settlement of disputes, which are likely to impact them as much as Allies, and engage them on issues related to new threats and challenges. Potential areas of common interest include the Libyan crisis, energy security, proliferation, and missile defense to name but a few. NATO does not need a formal partnership arrangement to generate a productive working dialogue with emerging powers and potential new partners. It does, however, need to take advantage of opportunities for dialogue, such as the upcoming NATO Summit in Chicago, as well as opportunities for collaboration when they arise.[45] The People's Republic of China, for instance, has participated alongside units from allied countries in the course of UN peace operations and antipiracy patrols around the Gulf of Aden already. Some countries in Central and South Asia have a major stake in maintaining stability in the Middle East and North Africa, which is known in China as West Asia. There is sufficient flexibility within NATO partnerships' policy, tools, and mechanisms to allow for their participation, be it on an ad hoc basis or making use of flexible formats to develop both political dialogue and military-to-military cooperation through a "variable geometry" approach. The real question is whether there will be political will to engage on their part and sufficient effort on the part of Allies to reach out to countries who may not share the same values as those of the Alliance and its current partners.

As the United States prepares to host the next NATO summit, back-to-back with the G8 Summit, it may consider ways to enrich the transatlantic partnership embodied in NATO and reach out to emerging powers in an effort to bring together America, Europe, and Asia in a broader security dialogue to address common challenges and develop common responses. This would be particularly relevant at a time when the American public and Congress seem to focus increasingly beyond Europe. The NATO-led operation in Libya could be an opportunity to develop such a broader security dialogue, as productive relationships with other countries and organizations will continue to enable NATO to be better informed, more capable, better prepared, and smarter at what it does. The post–Cold War era created an opportunity for NATO to reach out to former adversaries as they indicated an interest in partnering with the Alliance. Today's emerging powers and emerging security challenges present NATO with new opportunities for reaching out beyond its comfort zone, beyond those who think alike and share the same values. Allies will have to remain outward-looking and show increased flexibility to meet the security challenges of the 21st century.

Notes

[1] North Atlantic Treaty Organization (NATO), *NATO 2020: Assured Security; Dynamic Engagement* (Brussels: NATO Public Diplomacy Division, May 2010), available at <www.nato.int/strategic-concept/expertsreport.pdf>.

[2] NATO, "Active Engagement, Modern Defence," November 19, 2010, 2, para. 4, available at <www.nato.int/lisbon2010/strategic-concept-2010-eng.pdf>.

[3] NATO, "Lisbon Summit Declaration," November 20, 2010, available at <www.nato.int/cps/en/natolive/official_texts_688828.htm?mode=pressrelease>.

[4] Ibid., para. 27.

[5] NATO, "Active Engagement in Cooperative Security: A More Efficient and Flexible Partnership Policy," April 15, 2011, available at <www.nato.int/nato_static/assets/pdf/pdf_2011_04/20110415_110415-Partnership-Policy.pdf>.

[6] Since the early days of NATO partnerships in 1994 with the creation of Partnership for Peace (PfP), a distinction has been made between Partners, on the one hand, referring to countries who formally joined PfP and have been sitting in the Euro-Atlantic Cooperation council from Northern, Eastern and Central Europe, as well as the Caucasus and Central Asia at a later stage, and partners, on the other hand, referring to all other countries who cooperated with NATO in looser formats, such as the Mediterranean Dialogue and the Istanbul Cooperation Initiative, from North Africa to the Middle East. Over the years, NATO also reached out to countries outside the Euro-Atlantic area contributing to allied missions, often referred to as "operational partners" but also as "partners across the globe" effectively partnering with NATO outside any formal partnership arrangement such as PfP. These partners from Japan, New Zealand, Australia, and the Republic of Korea pledging troops and committing financial contributions to NATO-led operations were not only "partners of need," but also "partners of values" as well-established democracies. In Berlin, Allies opted for a more flexible approach to partnerships where the distinction between partners and Partners is slowly fading away. While the specificity of each partnership should remain politically significant, NATO will be able to manage partnership resources according to new political priorities as they emerge and reach out beyond current partnerships, no longer limited by the bureaucratic constraints of formal and informal frameworks of cooperation. In this paper, the term *partner* is used to refer to all NATO partners irrespective of their frameworks. All partners are yet qualified by their geographical origins.

[7] Following the popular uprising that began in Benghazi on February 17, 2011, the United Nations Security Council (UNSC) adopted Resolution 1970 and referred the situation in Libya to the International Criminal Court (ICC). The UNSCR instituted an arms embargo, froze the personal assets of Libya's leaders, and imposed a travel ban on senior figures. NATO stepped up its surveillance operations in the Central Mediterranean. NATO Defense Ministers met on March 10 and supported the Supreme Allied Commander Europe decision to have Alliance ships move to the same area to boost the monitoring efforts. On March 17, the UNSC adopted Resolution 1973, authorizing member states and regional organizations to take, inter alia, "all necessary measures" to protect civilians in Libya. NATO members immediately followed the UN call by launching a NATO-led operation to enforce the arms embargo against Libya, and began enforcing the embargo on March 23. In addition, on March 24, NATO decided

to enforce the UN-mandated no-fly zone over Libya given the UNSCR call for a ban on all flights except those for humanitarian and aid purposes to avoid air attacks from Libyan authorities perpetrated on civilians inside the country. Finally, on March 27, Allies agreed to take on the whole military operation in Libya under UNSCR 1973, taking over from a coalition led by the United States, France, and the United Kingdom, which had intervened militarily in the early days of the Libyan crisis. The purpose of the NATO-led Operation *Unified Protector* has served to protect civilians and civilian-populated areas under threat of attack. It was decided that the Alliance would implement all military aspects of the UN resolution. NATO effectively took action as part of the broad international effort and immediately indicated its desire to work with its partners in the region.

[8] It should be emphasized that the NATO-led operation gained the necessary legitimacy first through UNSCR 1973, which provided a sound legal basis, and second, through the support of the Arab League, which gave the necessary political support within the region for NATO to ultimately take the decision to intervene militarily. Without the support of the Arab League, the UNSC might not have been able to avoid the veto of some of its members. Furthermore, Allies would have been hard pressed to intervene in the region without support among Arab countries. Building on this original support from the Arab League, NATO was able to reach out to countries in the region and consult as it deployed Operation *Unified Protector*, making best use of its own partnership mechanisms in the region.

[9] The Mediterranean Dialogue (MD) framework was developed and agreed in 1994 and counts today seven countries bordering the Mediterranean who decided to enter into a partnership with NATO: Algeria, Egypt, Israel, Jordan, Mauritania, Morocco, and Tunisia. Jordan joined in late 1995 and Algeria only in 2000.

[10] The Istanbul Cooperation Initiative (ICI) framework was launched in 2004 at the Istanbul Summit and counts four Gulf countries. Bahrain, Kuwait, and Qatar joined the ICI in 2004, and the United Arab Emirates joined in 2005.

[11] The ICI and MD had often been criticized for moving slowly in the area of defense-military cooperation, favoring instead public diplomacy projects and thus characterized as "a diplomatic talking shop." See Helle Malmvig, "From a Diplomatic Talking Shop to a Powerful Partnership? NATO's Mediterranean Dialogue and the Democratisation of the Middle East," Danish Institute for International Studies Brief, May 2004. From the onset, these frameworks of cooperation were mainly supported by Italy and Spain within the Alliance, both supportive of a broader role for NATO in the face of security challenges coming from the South. See Domenico Corcione, "New Risks and Roles in NATO's Southern Region," *NATO's Sixteen Nations*, no. 93 (1993), 37–39.

[12] Two countries in the region were able to contribute militarily to Operation *Unified Protector*, Qatar and UAE, while Jordan provided staff and analytical support. Other partners such as Sweden also contributed militarily to the operation. Malta provided significant support to NATO for the air and naval operations.

[13] The NATO Secretary-General delivered a speech on June 16, 2011, in the Spanish Senate where he stated that "These changes were totally unexpected. And they were momentous. They bring new responsibilities for NATO. And they bring new hope for millions of people." In this speech, the Secretary-General argues for increased cooperation with southern partners in the area of practical cooperation and political dialogue. See <www.nato.int/cps/en/natolive/opinions_75547.htm>. It is also

interesting to note that for his part, the Russian representative to NATO, Ambassador Dimitry Rogozin, has interpreted the recent events and the NATO-led operation in Libya as "the beginning of NATO's expansion to the south." This may actually be a sign that Russia will finally soften its position vis-à-vis NATO enlargement eastward. It may also indicate yet another area of discord whereby Moscow will now direct its criticism of the Alliance toward NATO's approach to security in its southern dimension.

[14] In 1994, MD was ushered in by some Allies who were somewhat uneasy about NATO moving east. The Alliance traditionally had little interest south of the Mediterranean, which was left to bilateral relations between countries on both sides. In fact, a number of Allies were leery of any possibilities to see NATO dragged into the Arab-Israeli conflict. See Gareth Winrow, *Dialogue with the Mediterranean: The Role of NATO's Mediterranean Dialogue* (New York: Garland Publishing, 2000), 44–68.

[15] The NATO heads of state and government in Lisbon have "agreed to further enhance our existing partnerships and to develop new ones with interested countries and organizations" (NATO, "Lisbon Summit Declaration," para. 2). Moreover, in paragraph 25, it is stated that "NATO's relationships with other partners across the globe are expanding and deepening, reflecting common goals in the area of security." While in paragraph 26, the declaration calls to "better engage with our partners across the globe who contribute significantly to security, and reach out to relevant partners to build trust, increase transparency and develop practical cooperation." Finally, the declaration in the same paragraph calls on Allies to "develop flexible formats to discuss security challenges with our partners and enhance existing fora for political dialogue." This was essentially language aimed at reaching out to countries outside of existing NATO partnership frameworks and seeking to engage significant contributors to security—countries that some have also called "significant security interlocutors." Unable at this stage to develop consensus around the identity of these countries, one often sees in speeches and various documents a couple of countries regularly listed as examples: China, India, and South Africa. At times, Brazil, Russia, India, China, and South Africa are also mentioned informally.

[16] In this paper, the term *south* is often used in a generic sense without precise geographical delineation. It refers to the broad region extending from North Africa, where NATO already counts seven partners, to the Gulf region, where NATO has established relations with four partner countries. The paper avoids referring to the Middle East given the sensitivities within the Alliance to any potential NATO role in the Middle East peace process (see note 14). This constitutes one of the inherent limits of NATO's potential role south of the Mediterranean.

[17] On June 8, 2011, NATO Defense Ministers "have extended Operation Unified Protector for a further 90 days from 27 June." See NATO, "Statement on Libya, 8 June 2011," available at <www.nato.int/cps/en/natolive/news_75177.htm>.

[18] See "Split in Nato over Libya mission," March 22, 2011, available at <http://nation.com.pk/pakistan-news-newspaper-daily-english-online/Politics/22-Mar-2011/Split-in-Nato-over-Libya-mission>; David Brunnstrom, "NATO still split on taking over Libya operation," March 23, 2011, available at <http://uk.mobile.reuters.com/article/worldNews/idUKTRE72M4T720110323?feedType=RSS&feedName=worldNews>; Steven Lee Myers and David D. Kirkpatrick, "Allies are split on goal and exit strategy in Libya," *The New York Times*, March 25, 2011, available at <www.nytimes.com/2011/03/25/world/africa/25policy.html?_r=1&scp=12&sq=25%20march%202011&st=cse>.

[19] On April 14, Foreign Ministers in Berlin agreed to three goals yet unachieved and justifying the renewed mandate by Defense Ministers on June 8: that the Libyan regime cease attacks on civilians;

that the regime withdrew its forces to bases; and that immediate, full, and safe unhindered humanitarian access was achieved. These goals actually reiterated what was already in UNSCR 1970 and 1973.

[20] "Libya: NATO chief vows to continue war dispite [sic] split over it," June 23, 2011, available at <http://realisticbird.wordpress.com/2011/06/23/libya-nato-chief-vows-to-continue-war-dispite-split-over-it/>.

[21] The German Marshall Fund explains the positions of some allied countries in Libya through public opinion support. See "Coordinate the Means but Not the Ends—Justifying U.S. and European Intervention in Libya," available at <http://blog.gmfus.org/2011/04/coordinate-the-means-but-not-the-ends—justifying-u-s-and-european-intervention-in-libya>.

[22] On March 29 at the initiative of the British Foreign Secretary, the London Conference took place and gathered 40 Foreign Ministers and representatives from key regional organizations and leaders. The London Conference marked an important step with the decision that the North Atlantic Council would provide executive political direction to NATO operations. It marked also the establishment of the Libyan Contact Group, which was to provide the overall political direction and leadership on behalf of the international community. This was the forum for coordination of the overall international response to Libya and met for the first time in Doha, Qatar, on April 13.

[23] The opposition movement to Qadhafi—the "rebels" also known as the Transitional National Council (TNC)—has been recognized by an increasing number of countries as the legitimate representation of the Libyan people. The international community remains cautious, however, in its support. A lack of trust preventing full-scale support toward the TNC lingers and stems from existing elements within the council with prior connections to the Qadhafi regime and other elements harboring potential jihadist ideals. Without a viable opposition, however, able to safeguard territorial integrity and represent the whole of Libya, the international community would be hard pressed to support a final settlement. Caution was recently heightened in the face of obvious splits within the TNC and unclear linkages with the Qadhafi forces in the context of the recent murder of TNC General Abdel Fattah Younes. See M.S., "Libya's rebel forces: Bad news from Benghazi," July 29, 2011, available at <www.economist.com/blogs/newsbook/2011/07/libyas-rebel-forces>. There is however no alternative to the TNC to deliver the necessary political transition today in post-Qadhafi Libya. Nonetheless, the international community is yet to see a legitimate and unified opposition to take Libya forward beyond the current transition period.

[24] On May 16, 2011, the International Criminal Court prosecutor asked the judges of the court to issue arrest warrants for three suspects for crimes against humanity, including Qadhafi. Seeking an exit strategy for Qadhafi and his entourage has not been made any easier by this indictment, which has left him with little options and motivation to consider any negotiated settlement. See George Friedman, "Libya and the problem with The Hague," July 11, 2011, available at <www.stratfor.com/weekly/20110711-libya-and-problem-hague?ip_auth_redirect=1>.

[25] At the Bucharest Summit in April 2008, NATO heads of state and government endorsed a set of pragmatic proposals to develop and implement NATO's contribution to a comprehensive approach. The idea was to enhance Alliance contribution to civil-military cooperation in delivering stabilization and reconstruction to countries marred by conflicts and facing considerable challenges in coordinating the efforts from the international community involved in crisis management. Building on earlier

efforts at the Lisbon Summit in 2010, NATO heads of state and government in their declaration (para, 2) "decided to enhance NATO's contribution to a comprehensive approach to crisis management, as part of the international community's effort and to improve NATO's ability to deliver stabilization and reconstruction effects." To that end, they "agreed to form an appropriate but modest civilian capability to interface more effectively with other actors and conduct appropriate planning in crisis management." See NATO, "Lisbon Summit Declaration," para. 9.

[26] Ibid., para. 8.

[27] On June 8, 2011, at his press conference following the meeting of NATO Defense Ministers with non-NATO contributing nations to Operation *Unified Protector*, the Secretary-General stated, "We agreed that the time has come to plan for the day after the conflict. Qaddafi's history, it is no longer a question of if he goes, but when he goes. It may take weeks, but it could happen tomorrow. And when he goes the international community has to be ready. Let me make it clear. We do not see a leading role for NATO in Libya once this crisis is over. But we are ready to engage with other international and regional organizations to ensure a smooth transition." Available at <www.nato.int/cps/en/natolive/opinions_75176.htm>.

[28] For insights on the various developments within MD and ICI over the past 15 years and their inherent limits, see Vivien Pertusot, *NATO Partnerships: Shaking Hands or Shaking the System?* Focus Strategique no. 31 (Paris: IFRI Security Studies Center, May 2011), 20–22.

[29] While NATO agreed to intervene in Libya, the crisis in Bahrain was dealt with differently. The wind of change—which swept notably Tunisia, Egypt, Bahrain, Libya, Yemen, and Syria engulfing the whole region—in the past few months prompted the Saudi-led Gulf Cooperation Council to intervene militarily in mid-March at the request of the Bahraini royal family. The uprising on the island shook the Arab monarchies of the Persian Gulf, who reached out and multiplied demarches and quiet diplomacy to inform the international community and to seek help in addressing the challenges facing the Bahraini regime. The region was at risk of facing Shia-led movements possibly exploited by Iran and thereby threatening the whole Eastern Arabia and Saudi Arabia's oil rich eastern province. See "The Greater Game in Bahrain," June 29, 2011, available at <www.stratfor.com/geopolitical_diary/20110628-greater-game-bahrain>. This intervention showed that military capabilities and resources could be sufficient to address crises from within the region. Future crises may therefore be dealt from within the region. In that context, there may be scope for NATO to provide assistance in building capability rather than intervening militarily.

[30] See "Putin likens Libya air strikes to 'crusades,'" March 21, 2011, available at <www.telegraph.co.uk/news/worldnews/africaandindianocean/libya/8396746/Putin-likens-Libya-air-strikes-to-crusades.html>.

[31] See "Medvedev: Putin's Statement on Libya 'Inadmissible,'" March 21, 2011, available at <http://russian-law.livejournal.com/59429.html>.

[32] Full transcript of Sergey Lavrov interview, June 1, 2011, available at <www.ln.mid.ru/bdomp/brp_4.nsf/e78a48070f128a7b43256999005bcbb3/bb345b48652d15e7c325782c002f506c!OpenDocument>.

[33] "Russia Chess Match in Libya," June 15, 2011, available at <www.stratfor.com/geopolitical_diary/20110614-russias-chess-match-libya>.

[34] Lavrov interview. Among the G8 countries at the Deauville Summit, Russia was apparently the only player keeping contacts with both Tripoli and Benghazi.

[35] See reference to this meeting at <www.nato.int/cps/en/natolive/news_76039.htm?>.

[36] In NATO, *smart defense*—a concept presented at the Munich Security Conference on February 4, 2011—aims at building security for less money by working together and being more flexible, so as to "spend better" knowing that Allies will not be spending more in the short term. See NATO Secretary-General Anders Fogh Rasmussen, Keynote Speech, "Building security in an age of austerity," available at <www.nato.int/cps/en/natolive/opinions_70400.htm>.

[37] Robert M. Gates, "The Future of NATO," June 10, 2010, available at <www.defense.gov/speeches/speech.aspx?speechid=1581>.

[38] NATO Secretary-General Anders Fogh Rasmussen, "NATO after Libya," June 29, 2011, available at <www.nato.int/cps/en/natolive/opinions_75836.htm>.

[39] John E. Herbst and Leo G. Michel, "Why the EU should patrol Libya," *European Voice*, July 14, 2011, 9.

[40] Rasmussen, "NATO after Libya."

[41] China dispatched a military vessel and planes to the region to evacuate its citizens, while Russia sent a presidential envoy in a mediating effort to broker a political settlement in Libya.

[42] NATO Secretary-General Anders Fogh Rasmussen, "NATO and the Mediterranean: The Changes Ahead," June 16, 2011, available at <www.nato.int/cps/en/natolive/opinions_75547.htm>.

[43] The NATO Secretary-General argues for closer European Union–NATO cooperation in this regard. See Rasmussen, "NATO after Libya."

[44] NATO, *NATO 2020: Assured Security; Dynamic Engagement*, 10.

[45] It may be that in the context of the Chicago Summit, the focus of attention on NATO-led missions will be exclusively and purposely on Afghanistan and that the Allies, including the host nation, will refrain from adding yet another meeting for Operation *Unified Protector*. This should still present an opportunity to reach out to emerging powers in the context of Afghanistan post-transition.

About the Author

Dr. Isabelle François is a Distinguished Senior Visiting Research Fellow in the Center for Transatlantic Security Studies, Institute for National Strategic Studies, at the National Defense University. She served previously at North Atlantic Treaty Organization (NATO) Headquarters as Head of Euro-Atlantic Integration and Partnership. From 1998 to 2011, she held various positions on the NATO International Staff, including Director of NATO Information Office in Moscow (2004–2009). She received the Medal of Excellence from the NATO Secretary-General in 2007 for a significant public diplomacy event—the 2006 NATO-Russia Rally—organized in the Russian Federation. She has worked within the Alliance on a range of issues dealing with NATO partnerships and outreach policy. Before joining the Alliance, she served at the Department of National Defence (DND) from 1993 to 1998 in the Policy Group, both within the NATO Directorate (1996–1998) and Directorate of Strategic Analysis (1993–1996), where she published extensively on defense issues related to Africa and Europe. She then took a more operational assignment as part of the team in charge of drafting the 1994 Canadian Defense White Paper. Dr. François holds a Law Degree from Université de Paris XII (France) and is a graduate of Carleton University (MA) in Ottawa, Ontario, and Université de Montréal (Ph.D.) in Québec.